Sell Forever

Andrew Howard

Andrew Howard

Copyright Page

Index

The Fundamentals of a Solid Business

The foundation of any business is what will determine whether it will have the strength to survive the test of time. A solid business is one that is built from day one with a clear and firm foundation, and that begins with three fundamental elements: the company's mission, vision, and values. These are not just pretty words for a website or to impress customers; they are the essence that will guide all decisions, strategies, and actions throughout the life of the business.

The mission is the heart of the business. It is the "why" of your existence, the reason why you get up every day to work. Defining a clear mission means asking yourself: what problem do I want to solve? Who do I want to help? Why am I here? This statement must be authentic and deeply connected to what you want to achieve. Think of great brands that have transcended generations; they all have clear missions. It is not just about selling products, but about creating a positive impact. A business that knows why it exists can withstand the winds of change, because it will always find a way to adapt without losing its essence.

Vision, on the other hand, is "where" the business is headed. A strong vision looks into the future with a clear idea of what the company wants to achieve in the coming years, even decades. It's like imagining the final destination on a journey. Having a clear vision is critical because it motivates and guides both the business owner and the entire team. When you have an inspiring vision, difficult days become more manageable because you know there is a big, meaningful goal worth achieving. Plus, a powerful vision has the ability to attract people who share that dream, whether they are employees, customers, or business partners.

Now, values are the "how" that path is to be followed. They are the rules of the game, the principles that determine the actions and behaviors within the business. Values are what shape the company culture. For example, if one of the values is honesty, then all business practices will be oriented towards transparency and ethics. If innovation is valued, then there will always be a desire to improve and be at the forefront, no matter how many years pass. Strong values allow difficult decisions to be made when the road gets tough and help maintain consistency over time. A business that operates with clear values generates trust in customers and builds deeper, longer-lasting relationships.

Without these three fundamental elements, a business lacks direction. It's like building a house without a foundation; it may look good for a while, but sooner or later, the weight and adverse conditions will make it collapse. Having a clear mission, an inspiring vision, and strong values not only gives a business an identity, but also makes it storm-proof. Because, let's face it, building a business that lasts more than 100 years is not easy. It requires focus, commitment, and above all, clarity on what you want to achieve.

Furthermore, these fundamentals should not be static; they need to evolve over time. The market changes, customers change, and sometimes even personal goals change. Mission, vision, and values should be reviewed periodically to ensure they remain aligned with the direction of the business. But be careful, this does not mean changing them every time something goes wrong. It is more about adapting them, finding new ways to apply those same principles as the business grows and faces new challenges.

A common mistake is to think that these elements are only for large companies. On the contrary, the smaller and younger the business, the more vital it is to define them from the start. The mission, vision and values become a compass that guides every decision: from the type of products sold to the way customers are served. When clearly stated, they help avoid unnecessary detours and keep the focus on what really matters.

In short, the foundations of a solid business are not about magic formulas or following rigid rules. They are about deeply understanding why you want to do what you do, where you want to go, and how you want to navigate that path. This well-established foundation will allow the business to adapt, evolve, and, above all, endure beyond the whims of the market and passing fads. In the history of the longest-running businesses, there is always a common thread: they all have a clear mission, an inspiring vision, and solid values that have guided their path for decades.

Knowing Your Market Thoroughly

For a business to remain strong and relevant for more than 100 years, it is essential to know the market like the back of your hand. Often, companies focus so much on what they want to sell that they forget about what is most important: the people they are going to sell to. Understanding the market thoroughly is the key to creating products or services that are truly needed and, most importantly, that continue to be needed over time. It is not just about knowing who the customers are, but also anticipating their needs and desires, even before they themselves identify them.

The first step to understanding your market is research, research, research. Doing a market analysis doesn't just mean reading a few reports or surveys; it means immersing yourself in the world of your potential customers. What problems do they face in their daily lives? What excites them? What causes them concern? Knowing your market thoroughly means understanding these questions in depth, as customers can't always directly express what they need. That's why you have to learn to observe and listen beyond what they say.

A good way to start is to clearly define who you want to serve. Often, you want to reach everyone, but in reality, the strongest and most successful businesses are those that find a specific niche. This group of people, with specific needs and characteristics, is the one to whom you can offer unique value. The trick is to identify that niche, understand its particularities, and adapt to its needs. For example, if you want to sell sportswear, you have to ask yourself: who is it for? For beginner runners? For professional athletes? Each group has different needs, and knowing those differences is what will allow you to offer something that really resonates with them.

Another important aspect is analyzing your competition. This doesn't mean obsessing over what everyone else is doing, but rather understanding what they're offering, what's working for them, and what's not. By looking at your competition, you can learn about mistakes to avoid and opportunities to take advantage of. For example, if all businesses in the same industry are targeting a specific type of customer, there may be a group of people that aren't being served.

That could be the perfect niche to explore. Additionally, studying your competition helps you identify what's already out there in the market and how you can differentiate your business.

But knowing your market isn't a process you do once and forget about. Markets are constantly changing: new trends emerge, technologies evolve, and customer expectations shift. That's why you need to stay alert and keep researching, even when your business is doing well. A common mistake is thinking you know your market just because you've had good results for a while. Complacency is the enemy of longevity. To build a business that lasts more than a century, you need to be in a constant state of learning and adapting.

A valuable tool in this process is direct feedback from customers. Asking them what they like, what they would like to improve, and what other needs they have can be a goldmine of information. Often, customers are the ones who come up with the most innovative ideas for new products or services. Actively listening to customers and taking their feedback seriously shows that you value them and are willing to evolve to meet their expectations. This close connection with the market is what will allow you to adjust course when necessary and always stay relevant.

In addition to knowing your customers and competitors, it is essential to understand global trends affecting the market. Economic, social, cultural and technological changes can influence consumer behaviour and preferences. For example, in recent years there has been an increasing demand for ecological and sustainable products. Companies that anticipated this trend and adapted their products and processes to it have a strong position in the market today. Knowing and anticipating these trends allows businesses to adapt in time and avoid becoming obsolete.

The key is to be proactive, not reactive. It is not enough to respond to what the market demands today; you have to anticipate what it will demand tomorrow. This is achieved by staying informed, trying out new ideas, and experimenting with different strategies. Companies that last for generations are those that not only meet the current needs of their market, but also stay ahead of changes. This way, when fads or trends fade, the business has already found a way to evolve and remain relevant.

But what happens if, after all this analysis, it turns out that the market changes radically? Well, this is where the importance of being flexible comes into play. While knowing the market is essential, you also have to be willing to pivot when circumstances require it. Many companies have had to completely reinvent themselves to adapt to new realities, and that's not a bad thing; it's part of a healthy business. The important thing is not to lose sight of who your customers are and how you can continue to serve them in the best way possible.

In short, knowing your market inside out is like having a treasure map. This knowledge allows you to make informed decisions, spot opportunities, minimize risks and, above all, build a business that stays relevant over time. It's not about predicting the future accurately, but rather being prepared to adapt and evolve with changes in the environment. Companies that know their market well are those that manage to establish long-lasting relationships with their customers, creating a solid foundation to grow and prosper for generations. So, never stop researching, learning and adapting; it's the only way to build a business that truly lasts forever.

The Product as a Fundamental Pillar

The product is, without a doubt, the fundamental pillar of any business. You can have the best sales strategy, the most brilliant marketing, and the most talented team, but if your product fails to meet customer expectations, the business is destined to fail. The product is the reason why the customer chooses your company over others and it is what makes them come back again and again. It is the foundation on which the entire brand reputation is built and therefore it is essential that it is of the highest quality and that it actually solves a problem or fulfills a customer need.

For a product to be strong and able to stand the test of time, it must have a unique value that makes it stand out in the market. It's not just about offering something that already exists, but about making it better, more efficient, more attractive, or simply different in a way that connects with people. Originality is key, but it doesn't always mean reinventing the wheel. Sometimes, the most successful products are those that take an existing idea and improve it or adapt it for a specific group of people. The point is to find that "something" that makes your product special and, at the same time, difficult for others to replicate.

Another crucial aspect is product quality. This may sound obvious, but many companies fall into the trap of cutting costs on materials or processes to make more profits in the short term, forgetting that quality is what builds customer trust. A quality product is one that delivers what it promises. If you sell something that wears out easily, doesn't work as it should, or simply doesn't live up to expectations, it's only a matter of time before customers start looking for alternatives. That's why investing in quality is a safe bet for the future. A well-made product doesn't just sell once, it creates a loyal customer who will return and recommend your business to others.

But quality isn't just about materials or function; it's also about the experience the product offers. From packaging to customer service, every detail counts. The experience of using your product should be so good that it leaves a positive impression in the customer's mind. Think about it: most purchasing decisions are based on emotions. If the customer feels that your product brings them satisfaction, comfort, or even a little joy, they will become an ambassador for your brand. People don't just buy products; they buy experiences. Take care of every aspect of that experience, and your product will become a pillar that will sustain the business for decades.

Another key to building a product as a fundamental pillar is constant innovation. The market changes, customer needs evolve, and what is popular today may not be so tomorrow. That is why your product must be in a continuous process of improvement. This does not mean radically changing it all the time, but rather looking for ways to make it more useful, easier to use, or more attractive. Innovation can be something as simple as a new design, additional functionality, or an improvement in presentation. The important thing is that the product does not become stagnant. Even the most successful products need to be updated to stay relevant. The businesses that manage to stay around for more than 100 years are those that have known how to reinvent their products over and over again, without losing the essence that makes them unique.

With this in mind, it is essential to always be attentive to customer feedback. They are the ones who use the product and who can offer the best ideas for improving it. Sometimes, small details that go unnoticed by the creator are the ones that matter the most to users. Actively listening and adapting to customer suggestions not only improves the product, but also shows that you care about offering them the best. This attitude generates loyalty and strengthens the relationship with consumers, creating a community around the product that is difficult to break.

Now, we need to talk about product adaptability. No matter how good it is, it needs to be able to adapt to changes in the market. This may mean adjusting the design, changing materials, or even transforming the product entirely. A solid business is one that doesn't blindly cling to an idea, but is willing to evolve over time. For example, many companies that have endured for decades started out offering a very different product than the one they sell today. What has kept them relevant is their ability to adapt to new circumstances, always keeping quality and customer experience at the center.

Finally, it is important to remember that the product is the visible face of the business. It is the first thing that customers see and what remains in their memory after the purchase. Therefore, it is essential that the product reflects the values and mission of the company. If your business is based on sustainability, for example, your product must be aligned with that philosophy. If you promote inclusion, your product must be accessible to everyone. The coherence between the product and the company's values is what creates a solid and reliable brand, capable of resisting the onslaught of competition and passing fads.

In short, the product is much more than just an object or service; it is the soul of the business. Its quality, its unique value, the experience it offers and its ability to adapt to changes are the elements that make it the fundamental pillar of a company that can last more than 100 years. Investing in developing an excellent product, listening to customers and constantly improving it, is the surest way to build a solid foundation that sustains the business over time. Because in the end, a good product is the best advertising, the best sales strategy and the best legacy that a business can leave.

Sales Strategies That Stand the Test of Time

Sales strategies are the engine that drives any business. Without sales, there is no revenue, and without revenue, a business cannot grow, much less sustain itself for more than 100 years. But what types of strategies truly stand the test of time? The answer lies in those that focus on relationships, value, and adaptability. Sales fads come and go, but principles that are based on understanding and serving the customer, rather than just selling them something, are the ones that last.

For starters, one of the strongest and most long-lasting strategies is consultative selling. This means moving away from the traditional approach of just talking about product features and instead focusing on helping the customer solve a problem or fulfill a need. The key is to listen more than you talk. By understanding the customer's true needs, you can offer a solution that actually makes sense to them. Not only does this make selling more effective, it also builds a relationship of trust. Customers feel valued when they are treated like people and not just numbers. And a trusting customer is a customer who returns and recommends your business to others.

Another key strategy is added value. Customers want to feel like they are getting more than what they pay for, and that goes beyond the product itself. Offering added value means thinking about the entire customer experience. This can be anything from excellent customer service to extended warranties, additional resources like guides or tutorials, or simply friendly, personalized treatment. Added value is what differentiates a business from its competitors and what turns a simple transaction into a memorable experience. Plus, it is something that can be adapted and evolved over time. As customer expectations change, you can adjust what you offer as additional value to maintain satisfaction and interest.

Honesty and transparency are also part of sales strategies that stand the test of time. In a world where information is accessible with just a click, customers know when they are being told the truth and when they are not. Misleading or hiding details may yield a quick sale, but it almost always ensures that the customer will not return. That's why it's best to be clear from the beginning, explaining benefits, limitations, and pricing in a transparent manner. People appreciate sincerity and authenticity, and this creates a positive reputation that can last for decades. Businesses that have endured over the years are those that have always been honest, even when the news isn't the best.

One strategy that has proven effective over the years is building long-term relationships. A sale should not be seen as a one-time event, but rather as the beginning of an ongoing relationship with the customer. This means staying in touch, continuing to provide value even after the purchase, and letting the customer know they are taken into account. Loyalty programs, discounts for frequent customers, and follow-up campaigns are all effective ways to keep that relationship alive. But beyond specific strategies, what really counts is genuine engagement with the customer. By feeling valued and cared for, the customer will be more willing to continue buying from you and recommend your business to others.

Adaptability is another key feature of sales strategies that last. The market is constantly changing, customer preferences evolve, and new technologies appear all the time. That's why sales strategies need to be flexible and adjustable. It doesn't mean changing direction every time a new trend emerges, but rather being aware enough to spot what changes can improve the way you sell and how you interact with customers. For example, e-commerce has become an essential tool for sales. Adapting to this change and learning how to sell online can open up new opportunities and keep your business relevant in an increasingly digital world.

Still, there are classic strategies that always work. Word-of-mouth recommendations are one of them. No matter how much technology exists, nothing beats the trust that comes with a recommendation from a friend or family member. To foster this, you need to make sure you offer a product and service so good that customers want to talk about it. Additionally, you can encourage word-of-mouth by offering referral rewards or creating affiliate programs. The key is to create such a positive experience that customers become the best promoters of the brand.

Another strategy that has proven to be effective over time is storytelling. Stories connect emotionally with people and make the product or service more memorable. Instead of just talking about the features of the product, you can tell the story of how it was created, why it is important, or how it has helped others. Stories humanize the brand and allow customers to identify with it. In addition, they are a great way to convey the values of the business, which reinforces customer trust and loyalty.

Finally, one strategy that never fails is ongoing training for the sales team. People who are in direct contact with customers are the face of the business. Therefore, they must be trained not only in product features, but also in how to communicate effectively, how to listen, and how to adapt to different customer personalities. A well-trained and motivated sales team can make the difference between a sporadic sale and a long-lasting relationship with the customer. In addition, by investing in their training, you show them that they are valuable to the company, which increases their commitment and performance.

In short, sales strategies that stand the test of time are those that focus on the customer and deliver genuine value. It's not about gimmicks or passing tactics, but about building relationships based on trust, honesty, and continually adapting to changing market needs. Selling is about much more than closing a deal; it's an opportunity to create a lasting connection with people. By implementing strategies that prioritize that connection, your business will not only survive, but thrive for generations. Because at the end of the day, sales aren't just numbers; they're people choosing to trust your business again and again.

Marketing that Transcends

Marketing is the bridge between your product and your customers. No matter how amazing your offering is, if people don't know about it or understand its value, it will be difficult for them to buy it. Marketing that transcends is not simply advertising or an occasional social media campaign; it is a set of actions and messages that build the image of your business over time. It is the way your company presents itself to the world and how it connects with people. The goal is to create such a strong impact that it not only captures the attention of customers, but also inspires them to continue choosing your brand generation after generation.

To achieve marketing that transcends, the first thing is to define a solid brand identity. This goes far beyond having a nice logo or a good slogan. The brand identity is the personality of your business. Is it friendly, professional, innovative, approachable? What are the values it represents? What story does it tell? Answering these questions is key because, in a world full of options, customers often choose brands they identify with. A clear and consistent identity makes your business memorable and gives customers a reason to choose you over others.

Once you've defined your identity, the next step is to create an authentic message. Authenticity is crucial in marketing that transcends. People want to connect with brands that are honest and genuine, not those that are just looking to sell. That's why it's important to communicate not only what you offer, but why you offer it. Talk about the values that guide your business, how your product can improve people's lives, and the real stories behind what you do. The more authentic your message, the deeper the impact on customers, and that's what creates a lasting connection.

Consistency is another key piece of marketing that lasts. It doesn't matter if you're using social media ads, email campaigns, events, or any other channel; the message and style should be consistent. Consistency helps customers recognize your brand everywhere and gives them a sense of familiarity and trust. Businesses that maintain a consistent and uniform presence across all their marketing efforts are the ones that manage to create a strong image in people's minds. This doesn't mean being boring or repetitive, but rather having a clear line that guides all communications.

One key aspect of marketing that transcends is focusing on the customer experience. Marketing doesn't end when the customer makes a purchase; in fact, that's where it begins. Every interaction with your business is an opportunity to reinforce your brand message and build a long-term relationship. This includes customer service, the purchasing process, product quality, and even post-sale follow-up. A satisfied customer not only returns, but also becomes a brand advocate, recommending your brand to friends and family. The most effective marketing is the kind that is based on the real, positive experience people have with your business.

Creativity plays a huge role in marketing that transcends. In a world where people are exposed to thousands of messages every day, being creative is what will make your business stand out. It's not just about having eye-catching ads, but finding unique ways to communicate the value of what you offer. It can be through an emotional story, educational content that helps customers solve a problem, or an interactive experience that makes them feel a part of the brand. Creativity allows marketing to be memorable, and memorable is what stays in people's minds over time.

However, there is something that goes beyond creativity and authenticity: emotional connection. Marketing that transcends is that which manages to connect with people's emotions. Emotions are powerful, and when a customer feels that your brand understands them, inspires them or makes them feel good, a bond is created that is difficult to break. Therefore, marketing must focus on the emotional benefits of your product, on how it improves people's lives or how it makes them feel. The brands that achieve this are those that become part of their customers' lives, not just as a purchase option, but as something meaningful and valuable.

Another essential element is adaptability. Marketing that transcends doesn't get stuck in a single strategy. The world changes, trends come and go, and ways of communicating are constantly evolving.

Effective marketing is one that adapts to these changes without losing its essence. This means being open to trying new channels, such as emerging social media, exploring new forms of content, or adjusting the message so that it remains relevant to new generations. Adaptability allows marketing to always be fresh and appropriate, keeping the brand present in the minds of customers, no matter how their habits change.

The importance of content cannot be overlooked either. Content is the most effective way to educate customers, entertain them, and show them that you are an expert in your field. Articles, videos, tutorials, infographics, and social media posts are just a few forms of content that can help position your business as a market leader. Good content doesn't just focus on selling, but on providing value, answering questions, and solving problems. This builds trust and, over time, turns readers or viewers into loyal customers.

Finally, it is important to understand that successful marketing does not seek immediate sales, but rather relationship building. Campaigns that only seek quick results may generate temporary income, but those that focus on building a community are the ones that create a sustainable business. Community is the basis of long-lasting marketing. People want to be part of something bigger, they want to feel that they share values and interests with the brand. By creating a community around your business, you not only gain customers, but ambassadors who will carry your message beyond what any advertising campaign could achieve.

In short, marketing that transcends is based on authenticity, consistency, creativity and emotional connection. It is an ongoing process that involves clearly communicating who you are, what you offer and why customers should choose you. By focusing on customer experience, adapting to change and building lasting relationships, your marketing will not only capture people's attention, but also their hearts. And when you achieve this, your business becomes more than just a company; it becomes a brand that endures, transcends time and remains relevant for generations to come.

Building Customer Relationships

Building relationships with customers is one of the most important pillars for a business to last more than 100 years. Often, businesses focus so much on acquiring new customers that they forget how valuable it is to take care of the ones they already have. Customers are not just transactions; they are people with needs, expectations, and desires. When customers feel that a company truly values and cares about them, they become loyal customers. And loyalty is what drives a business to grow, even in difficult times.

The relationship with the customer begins long before the first sale. From the first moment a person comes into contact with your business, whether through a social media post, an advertisement or a referral, an impression is being formed. That's why it's important to always present a positive and open attitude. This includes being transparent about what you offer, showing interest in people's needs and offering help or information without expecting anything in return. The first impression is vital, because it can be the difference between a customer being attracted to your business or one passing by.

Once a customer decides to make their first purchase, that's where building a relationship really begins. Here, customer service plays a crucial role. Being friendly, answering questions clearly and quickly, and making the buying process smooth and enjoyable are details that customers will always remember. But customer service isn't limited to just the sale. After-purchase care is just as important. Asking the customer how the product went, if they have any questions, or if they need extra help shows that you care about more than just closing a sale. This attention to detail creates a positive experience that makes the customer want to come back.

Constant contact is another key to strengthening customer relationships. It's not about bombarding them with promotions or messages, but about staying present in a helpful and valuable way. A newsletter, updates on new products, tips related to using what they bought, or simply a special greeting on important dates like their birthday, are effective ways to maintain close communication. These kinds of details show the customer that they are not just a number for the business, but a person with whom you want to establish a real bond. And it is that bond that turns a casual customer into a loyal customer.

Listening is perhaps the most important part of relationship building. Often, businesses talk and talk about what they offer, but forget to listen to what customers actually need or think. Asking for customer feedback, whether through surveys, direct feedback, or in casual conversations, is essential to understanding their expectations and how you can improve. It's not just about getting praise; criticism is valuable, too. When a customer takes the time to point out a problem or make a suggestion, it means they care about your business enough to want it to improve. Appreciating and acting on that feedback strengthens the relationship and shows that the business is committed to delivering the best.

Personalization is another key aspect. We all like to feel special and unique, and customers are no exception. Offering personalized service, whether by remembering their preferences, recommending products that fit their needs, or calling them by name, creates a much more personal and human experience. Today, technology makes personalization easier, as it allows you to save data and details that can be useful in offering a more focused service. For example, if a customer always buys a certain type of product, you can inform them when there are new models or discounts. This type of action shows that you care about them and not just about selling.

Honesty and transparency are also essential in customer relations. If there is a problem with a product, a delay in a delivery, or any other inconvenience, it is best to be clear from the start. Customers do not like to be misled or feel that things are being kept from them. Explaining the situation, apologizing if necessary, and offering a solution or compensation not only resolves the problem, but also builds trust. People understand that mistakes can happen; it is how those mistakes are handled that makes the difference. A company that faces problems head on and is willing to resolve them earns the respect and loyalty of its customers.

It's also important to reward loyalty. Customers who have been with you for a long time deserve to feel special. Offering them exclusive discounts, early access to new products, surprise gifts, or rewards programs are effective ways to show appreciation for their patronage. These types of gestures not only make them feel valued, but also encourage them to continue choosing your business. In the end, it's about giving back a little of the support they've given you and reinforcing the idea that they're part of a community.

Building a community around the brand is another powerful strategy. Relationships aren't just between the business and each individual customer; it's also about connecting customers to each other. People enjoy feeling like they're part of something bigger, and a community provides that sense of belonging. This can be achieved by hosting events, creating online groups, or simply encouraging interaction between customers. A strong community not only supports the business, but also becomes a source of ongoing promotion and feedback. When customers feel like they're part of a community, they naturally advocate for the brand and recommend it.

Finally, it's important to remember that customer relationships need to be authentic. It's not about following a list of rules or applying manipulation techniques to get them to buy more. It's about genuinely caring about people, understanding them, and offering them the best. Authentic relationships are based on honesty, respect, and empathy. When a customer feels that the business treats them as a friend and not just a source of income, an emotional connection is created that is difficult to break. And it is that connection that can sustain a business for generations.

In short, building relationships with customers is a long-term investment. It involves listening to them, being present, being honest, offering personalized service, and creating a community. When a business focuses on people and not just sales, it creates a solid foundation that allows it to grow and sustain itself over time. Loyal customers don't just come back again and again; they also become ambassadors for the brand, recommending and sharing it with others. And that kind of loyalty is what really makes a business last for more than 100 years. Because, in the end, businesses are built with people, and the relationships with those people are what really matter.

Business Culture as a Basis for Success

Company culture is like the soul of a business. It's what defines who you are as a company, how you work, and how you interact with your customers. Many people think that culture is just a set of inspirational quotes hanging on the wall or a handbook given to employees on their first day. But true company culture goes much further than that. It's the sum of the values, beliefs, and behaviors that guide all decisions and actions within the company. Having a strong, positive culture not only impacts the work environment, but it's also key to the longevity and success of a business.

Imagine company culture as the roots of a tree. The deeper and stronger those roots are, the taller and more resilient the tree can grow. Likewise, a company with a strong culture can better weather market storms and challenges, stand firm, and continue to grow over time. This is because culture gives a company a sense of identity and a clear direction to follow. No matter how many changes there are in the environment, culture provides a framework for everyone in the company to know how to act and make decisions that are aligned with the business vision.

A good company culture starts with defining clear values. Values are those core principles that guide the behavior and decisions of everyone in the company. For example, a company might value honesty, innovation, quality, and customer service. These values aren't just nice words; they are commitments that the company makes on a day-to-day basis. When values are clear and lived authentically, they create a work environment where everyone knows what is expected of them and where the business is headed. This builds trust and unity, both among employees and with customers.

A fundamental aspect of company culture is how people are treated within the company. Employees are the heart of any business, and their well-being and satisfaction directly impact the quality of the product or service offered. A culture that values and cares for its employees creates a motivated, committed team that is willing to give their best. This means fostering an environment where ideas are heard, where effort is recognized, and where support is provided for personal and professional development. When employees feel valued and part of something important, it is reflected in their attitude, their productivity, and the way they treat customers.

Open communication is another key pillar of a successful company culture. Companies that thrive are those where information flows freely and where everyone, from managers to employees, feels comfortable sharing ideas, concerns, and suggestions. This creates an environment of transparency and trust that facilitates decision-making and problem-solving. An open communication culture also allows the company to be more agile and responsive to change, as everyone is informed and can quickly adapt to new circumstances. Communication is not just about talking, but also about listening. Companies that listen to their employees and customers build stronger relationships and become smarter, more resilient organizations.

Company culture is reflected in every detail of the business, from how projects are managed to how customers are served. For example, if the company values excellence, this will be seen in the quality of the product, in the attention to detail, and in the constant effort to improve. If it values innovation, it will encourage creativity, be open to new ideas, and not be afraid to experiment. And if it values integrity, it will behave honestly and ethically in all its interactions, whether with customers, suppliers, or employees. Culture is not something that can be faked; it is perceived in every action and is built over time through the consistency between what the company says and what it does.

An essential element of building a strong company culture is consistency. You can't preach certain values and then act contrary to them. For example, if your company says it values customer service, but then ignores complaints or treats customers indifferently, those values lose credibility. Consistency builds trust and sets a standard for behavior within the company. Leaders have a critical role to play in this regard, as they are primarily responsible for leading by example and embodying the values and principles of the company culture. When leaders act in accordance with the culture, they inspire others to do the same.

Company culture is also a determining factor in how a company deals with market challenges and changes. Businesses with a strong and adaptable culture tend to be more resilient because they have a mindset that encourages continuous learning, collaboration, and creativity in finding solutions. This doesn't mean they have all the answers, but they are willing to search, test, and adjust their strategies when necessary. A culture that promotes innovation and is not afraid of failure allows a company to evolve and stay relevant, no matter how quickly trends or external circumstances change.

Furthermore, company culture is a magnet for attracting and retaining talent. People want to work in a place where they feel aligned with the values and where they are given the opportunity to grow and contribute. A company with a good culture not only attracts top talent, but also motivates them to stay and do their best. This creates a positive cycle: motivated employees create a better work environment, which in turn improves the customer experience, leading to greater business success. All of this is made possible by a culture that fosters respect, collaboration, and commitment.

Finally, it is important to understand that company culture is not something that is built overnight. It requires time, effort and, above all, consistency. It is also an ongoing process that may need adjustments as the company grows and changes. The important thing is to stay true to the core values and be flexible to adapt without losing the essence. A strong culture is not static; it evolves with people and circumstances, but always keeps its core intact.

In short, company culture is the foundation upon which a business's long-lasting success is built. It is what defines how the company works, how it treats people, and how it responds to challenges. A positive and strong culture fosters a work environment where employees feel valued and motivated, which in turn is reflected in product or service quality and customer satisfaction. Consistency, open communication, and exemplary leadership are key to building and maintaining a culture that drives the business forward over the years. Because in the end, products and strategies may change, but culture is what truly defines a company and sets it up to last for more than 100 years.

Constant Innovation without Losing the Essence

Constant innovation is one of the most important factors for a business to survive and thrive over time. We live in a world that changes at an impressive speed: technology advances, consumer trends evolve and markets are continually transforming. To stay relevant and continue to grow, a company must always be willing to innovate, try new things and adapt to new realities. However, there is something fundamental in this process: innovating does not mean losing the essence of what makes your business special. Maintaining a balance between change and identity is what allows a company to succeed no matter how many years pass.

Often, when companies hear the word innovation, they automatically think of major technological revolutions or radical changes that completely transform their business model. While it is true that some innovations can be disruptive, more often than not innovation is about small, continuous improvements that make a difference. It is not always about reinventing the wheel; sometimes what a business needs is to optimize its processes, improve the customer experience, or adapt its products to better meet market needs. This ability to constantly improve is what keeps the business agile and prepared to face the changes that will inevitably arise.

The most important thing when innovating is to be clear about what makes the company unique. Every business has an essence, an identity that sets it apart from others. Maybe it's the unmatched quality of its products, the personalized service it offers, or the way it connects with its customers. That essence is the heart of the business, and it must remain intact even when looking for new ways to grow and improve. Innovating doesn't mean giving up what makes you special; it means finding ways to stay relevant without sacrificing your values and identity.

The key to successful innovation is to always keep the customer at the center. At the end of the day, any changes or improvements you make should be geared toward delivering a better customer experience. To do this, it's critical to listen to their feedback, pay attention to their needs, and observe how their behaviors change over time. The most effective innovations often arise from the very experiences and problems customers face. For example, if customers mention that they find it difficult to find certain information on your website, one innovation could be to redesign the page to make it clearer and easier to navigate. Sometimes, the simplest changes have the biggest impact.

Another way to innovate without losing your essence is to observe what other companies are doing, not to copy them, but to get inspired and find ideas that can be adapted to your own model. Businesses that survive and thrive are not afraid to learn from others and try different approaches. This does not mean giving up your identity, but rather enriching it with new perspectives. For example, if you see that other companies are using social media to better connect with their customers, you can explore how this tool could be integrated into your strategy without losing the tone and personality that characterizes your brand.

Fear of change is one of the biggest obstacles to innovation. Often, companies that have been successful for a long time can fall into the trap of thinking that if something has worked so far, there is no need to change it. However, this way of thinking can lead to stagnation. The reality is that markets change, and what worked ten or twenty years ago may not be effective today. Constant innovation is not just an option; it is a necessity to stay relevant. However, innovation does not mean changing everything at once or taking unnecessary risks. It is about experimenting, trying new ideas on a small scale, evaluating the results and adjusting as necessary.

A good way to encourage innovation within the business is to foster a culture that values creativity and experimentation. Employees, especially those who are in direct contact with customers, often have valuable ideas on how to improve products, processes or services. Creating an environment where everyone feels free to propose ideas and where failure is seen as a learning opportunity, rather than a failure, is essential for innovation to emerge naturally. A company that listens to its team and gives space to try new things is in a privileged position to adapt to changes and constantly improve.

However, innovation is not always about adding new things; sometimes it is about simplifying. Over time, businesses tend to accumulate processes, policies and products that, while once useful, can become obsolete or unnecessarily complex. Periodically reviewing what you are doing and asking yourself if it really brings value to the customer is an effective way to innovate. Eliminating what no longer works or updating it to be more effective can be just as important as creating something new. Simplicity can be a great source of innovation, as it makes the business more efficient and easier to manage.

Technology is certainly a great ally of innovation, but it is not the only one. Sometimes, the most significant changes come from adjusting the way you communicate with customers, changing your marketing approach or improving the shopping experience. For example, a small business can innovate by offering more personalized attention, making each customer feel unique and valued. Other businesses can find new opportunities by exploring different sales channels, such as online stores, local markets or partnerships with other companies. The important thing is to be creative and willing to try different things, always keeping the essence of the business as a guide.

Constant innovation also involves having a learning mindset. A business that sticks to what it already knows and doesn't seek to learn new things is destined to fall behind. This doesn't mean you should adopt every new trend that comes along, but rather be informed and open to new ideas that can benefit your business. Attending conferences, reading books, attending workshops, and talking to other entrepreneurs are all ways to stay up to date and find inspiration for new ideas. The more you learn, the more tools you have to innovate effectively.

In short, constant innovation is what allows a business to stay fresh, relevant and competitive over the years. But innovating doesn't mean losing your essence or changing what makes you unique. On the contrary, it's about finding new ways to enhance what you already do well, adapting to the changing needs of your customers and continually improving without sacrificing your identity. The key is to always be clear about who you are as a company and use that as a compass to guide your decisions. When you manage to innovate while maintaining your essence, your business becomes stronger, more adaptable and more prepared to face any challenge the future may bring.

Sustainable Financial Management

Sustainable financial management is the backbone of any business that aims to last more than a hundred years. For many entrepreneurs, talking about finances may seem boring or complicated, but it is a fundamental part of a company's survival and success. Managing money well means having control over income and expenses, knowing how to invest wisely and, above all, being prepared to deal with unforeseen events. When solid financial management is achieved, the business can grow steadily, overcoming crises and staying afloat for generations.

One of the first steps to sustainable financial management is having a clear budget. A budget is a plan that helps you see in detail how much money is coming in and going out of your business. Often, small businesses are run on a gut feeling basis, spending on what seems necessary and trusting that sales will continue to cover those expenses. This approach may work for a while, but it is not sustainable in the long term. A budget gives you a clear view of your financial situation and helps you make better decisions. For example, if you know how much you need to cover basic expenses, you can set more realistic sales goals and avoid going into unnecessary debt.

Controlling expenses is a fundamental part of financial management. It doesn't matter how much money your business is bringing in if you're spending more than you're earning. Many businesses, especially when they're just starting to become successful, fall into the trap of spending on things that aren't essential. Sure, investing in improvements and expansion is important, but doing so in a rush and without planning can put the stability of the business at risk. Before making any major expenditure, ask yourself: is it really necessary? Will it contribute to the growth of the business? Can I do it in a more economical way? Adopting a savings and efficiency mindset is crucial to maintaining a profitable and sustainable business.

In addition to controlling expenses, it is vital to build an emergency fund. An emergency fund is money that is set aside to cover unexpected or difficult situations, such as a drop in sales, an unexpected repair, or any problem that requires cash outlay. The life of a business is full of ups and downs, and having a financial cushion allows you to face those difficult times without seriously affecting your operation. Ideally, this fund should cover at least three to six months of basic expenses. This may seem difficult to achieve at first, but by allocating a small portion of your income regularly to this fund, over time it will become an invaluable safety net.

Another essential practice for sustainable financial management is to avoid excessive debt. Credits and loans can be useful for financing certain projects or investments, but it is important to use them with caution. Many companies take on excessive debt to expand quickly, only to find themselves with liquidity problems later on. Before applying for a loan, evaluate whether it is really necessary and whether your business can afford the payments without compromising other important areas. Ask yourself if there are alternatives, such as saving a little more before making the investment. The key is to make debt a strategic tool, not a burden that limits business operations.

As your business grows, it's essential to diversify your income as well. Relying on just one source of income can be risky, especially in rapidly changing markets. Diversification can be as simple as offering new products or services, exploring different sales channels, or even looking for investment opportunities outside of your core business. For example, if your business is in the business of selling products, you could diversify by creating online courses or offering services related to those products. The idea is not to put all your eggs in one basket. By diversifying, you reduce risk and create a stronger financial foundation.

Smart investment is another key piece of sustainable financial management. Rather than spending profits on luxuries or unnecessary expenses, it is more beneficial to reinvest some of them back into the business. This can include purchasing new machinery, developing a new product, training staff, or improving customer experience. Investing wisely means carefully evaluating options and choosing those that will truly add value and grow the business. Every investment should be viewed as a long-term bet, and it is important to have patience to see the results.

The importance of keeping detailed financial records should not be forgotten. Good financial control involves keeping an accurate record of all transactions: how much you sell, how much you spend, and what it is spent on. This is not only important for maintaining a clear picture of the business situation, but is also necessary for complying with tax obligations and making informed decisions. Today, there are many tools and software programs that make managing finances easier, so you don't need to be an accounting expert to keep good control. The important thing is to be disciplined and consistent in recording information.

Long-term financial planning is another essential aspect. Often, businesses focus only on the short term, on monthly sales goals or covering immediate expenses. However, sustainable financial management involves thinking about the future, about what you want your business to be like in five, ten, or twenty years. What do you need to get there? How much do you need to save or invest? What risks might you face and how could you prepare for them? Setting long-term financial goals gives you clear direction and helps you make decisions that are more aligned with sustainable business growth.

Finally, it is essential to continually learn and educate yourself about finances. The financial world can seem complicated, but understanding the basics is a huge advantage. Read books, take courses, consult experts if necessary. The more knowledge you have, the better prepared you will be to manage your resources and make sound decisions. Financial management is not something you learn overnight, but every step you take in the right direction will contribute to the strength and durability of your business.

In short, sustainable financial management is the art of managing resources intelligently, carefully and strategically. It is not about being extremely cautious or avoiding risks at all costs, but about having a clear vision, planning, controlling expenses and being prepared for the unexpected. It is about investing wisely, saving with discipline and diversifying to create a solid foundation. When finances are managed well, the business becomes more resilient and capable of overcoming crises, growing and staying strong over time. Because in the end, a business that takes care of its resources is a business that builds a future.

The Power of Diversification

Diversification is one of the most powerful strategies a business can adopt to ensure its long-term success. Simply put, diversification means not relying on a single source of income or a single product. It's like having multiple paths to the same destination: if one of those paths gets blocked, you always have other options to keep moving forward. This strategy is especially useful when circumstances change unexpectedly, such as an economic crisis, new competition, or changes in market trends. A business that diversifies becomes more resilient, flexible, and able to survive and thrive in almost any situation.

One of the most common ways to diversify is to offer different products or services. Imagine that your business sells just one product, for example, handmade candles. If, suddenly, interest in candles decreases or production costs skyrocket, your business could be in trouble. But if, in addition to candles, you offer other related products such as handmade soaps, essential oils or even candle-making workshops, you will be expanding your sources of income. This way, if one of the products loses popularity or faces difficulties, the others can help keep the business afloat. Diversification does not mean that you have to become a one-stop shop, but that you should find products or services that complement what you already offer and that appeal to your audience.

Another way to diversify is to explore new markets. Perhaps your business has focused on just one type of customer, for example, young people interested in eco-friendly products. However, there may be other markets that could also benefit from your products, such as families, businesses, or seniors. Broadening your focus to different consumer groups can increase your sales opportunities and reduce the risk of relying solely on one specific segment. Plus, selling into different markets allows you to learn more about the needs and preferences of various types of customers, which can inspire new ideas to improve and expand your offering.

Diversification can also involve creating new sales channels. Often, businesses are limited to just one channel, such as a physical store or a website. However, there are many other ways to reach customers, such as selling on social media, on e-commerce platforms, at local markets, or even through partnerships with other businesses. The more channels you use, the greater your chances of attracting new customers and generating more revenue. Additionally, having different sales channels can help you cope with difficult situations, such as when a physical store has to temporarily close or when a website experiences technical issues.

A very effective strategy for diversification is to offer different levels of products or services. For example, if you own a business that sells beauty products, you can create a premium line of products for those looking for a more upscale experience, while also offering a more affordable line for those on a budget. Not only does this tactic appeal to different types of customers, but it can also increase your profit margin. By giving your customers options, you allow them to choose what best fits their needs and preferences, which can increase their satisfaction and brand loyalty.

Another interesting aspect of diversification is exploring additional revenue streams that are not directly related to your core products or services. For example, if you have built a strong community of followers on social media or a blog, you may want to consider earning revenue through advertising, affiliations, or collaborations with other brands. Many businesses have found that sharing their knowledge and expertise can also be a profitable revenue stream. This can be done by offering online courses, in-person workshops, or even writing a book. The key is to identify what assets your business has and how you can leverage them to generate new revenue opportunities.

It's important to note that diversification doesn't mean abandoning what's already working well. In fact, the idea is to build on the foundations you've already established. If your business has a flagship product or an approach that has been successful, diversification should be a way to build on that success, not move away from it. The idea is to expand your offering in a way that is consistent with your brand's identity and values. For example, if your business is known for its focus on natural and organic products, any new product lines or services you offer should follow that same philosophy to maintain your customers' trust.

Now, diversifying doesn't mean you should rush into exploring all options at once. It's important to do your research and plan carefully before making any decisions. Ask yourself: What are the needs of my current customers? Is there a product or service that could complement what I already offer? What market trends can I take advantage of? What resources do I need to carry out this new initiative? Diversification should be a gradual and strategic process, focused on finding opportunities that can really add value to your business and your customers.

Diversification can also be a great way to strengthen your relationship with your customers. When you offer different options and products, you show them that you care about meeting their diverse needs and that you are willing to adapt to provide them with the best. Not only does this increase the chances of customers returning to buy, but it also makes your business harder for competitors to replace. A satisfied customer who finds a variety of solutions in your business will be more likely to stay with you and recommend you to others.

One of the common risks businesses face is getting stuck with a single product line that, while successful in the present, can become obsolete over time. Tastes and trends change, technology advances, and markets evolve. Diversification allows you to be prepared for those changes and gives you the flexibility to adapt to new circumstances without seriously affecting your business. It's not just about selling more stuff, but about building a more robust and adaptable business, capable of withstanding ups and downs and taking advantage of new opportunities that arise.

In short, diversification is a strategy that adds strength and stability to your business. By offering different products or services, exploring new markets, using various sales channels, and finding new sources of income, you ensure that you are not dependent on a single source and reduce the risks associated with market changes. Diversification allows you to expand your opportunities, connect with more customers, and create a structure that is more resilient to crises. It is not a process that should be done overnight or without proper planning, but with a careful and strategic approach, diversification can be the engine that drives your business to lasting success.

Developing an Unstoppable Sales Team

Developing an unstoppable sales team is key to building a strong, long-lasting business. At the end of the day, a business can have the best product, the best marketing strategies, and impeccable financial management, but if there isn't a team that can sell, all of those things lose value. A sales team is the engine that drives profits and growth. They are the people on the front lines, interacting with customers, representing the brand, and closing deals. A strong sales team not only sells, but also creates connections with customers, understands their needs, and builds brand loyalty. For your business to thrive for generations, you need a team that is competent, motivated, and above all, believes in what they are selling.

The first step to developing an unstoppable sales team is choosing the right people. It's often a mistake to think that anyone can sell, but the reality is that sales requires certain skills and attitudes. A good salesperson must be a good listener, someone who has empathy and can understand what the customer really needs. They also need to be a persistent person who is not easily discouraged by rejection. It's not just about hiring the people with the most experience or the best titles; it's about finding those who have the right attitude and are willing to learn and grow with the business. Hiring passionate people who truly identify with the company's mission and values will make a huge difference in the performance of the sales team.

Ongoing training is another key element of having a strong sales team. The world of sales changes all the time. Market trends evolve, customers become more demanding, and technologies transform the way we buy. That's why your sales team needs to be constantly learning. Offer regular training, whether it's in sales techniques, product knowledge, communication skills, or handling digital tools. When your team is well-informed, they can better answer customer questions, handle objections more confidently, and close deals more effectively. A well-trained sales team is also more trustworthy, as customers feel like they're dealing with people who know what they're talking about.

However, training should not only be about technical skills. It is also important to work on the personal development of each team member. Sales can be a challenging job, full of ups and downs. There are days when everything goes well and others when nothing seems to go as expected. That is why a good sales team needs to have a strong and resilient mindset. Promote activities that foster confidence, motivation and teamwork. Encourage your team to set personal goals and celebrate every achievement, no matter how small. Remember that a motivated and self-confident team is much more effective in their sales and in their ability to connect with customers.

Communication is another key aspect in developing an unstoppable sales team. A team that communicates well, both among themselves and with other departments in the company, can resolve issues faster and provide better service to customers. Organize regular meetings where everyone can share their experiences, discuss the challenges they face, and propose ideas. Listen to your team's suggestions and value them. Salespeople are in direct contact with customers, so they often have valuable insight into what works and what doesn't. When team members feel that their opinion counts, they feel more engaged and motivated to do their best.

It is also important to set clear and realistic goals for the sales team. Goals are a guide that helps focus efforts and measure progress. However, goals must be achievable and aligned with the overall objectives of the business. It is useless to set goals that are too high and only generate stress and frustration in the team. It is better to set gradual goals that can be met with effort and dedication, so that the team feels that they are making progress. In addition, goals must be specific, measurable and linked to a time frame. For example, instead of saying "increase sales", it would be more effective to say "increase sales by 10% in the next three months".

To keep a sales team going strong, recognition and rewards play a key role. Everyone wants to feel appreciated for their work, and the sales team is no exception. Recognize individual and team achievements, whether through words of appreciation, awards, or incentives. Rewards don't always have to be monetary; they can be days off, a special lunch, or even a simple thank you note. What's important is that the team feels like their efforts are appreciated and that they're working in a place where they're valued. This type of recognition fosters a positive and motivating environment, which drives salespeople to keep trying and improving.

Another crucial aspect is to offer ongoing support to your sales team. Often, salespeople face challenges such as difficult clients, constant rejections, or product issues. Instead of leaving them to deal with these problems alone, provide them with the support they need to overcome difficulties. This can include additional training, mentoring, or simply being there to listen and offer advice. A team that feels supported by the company will be more willing to face challenges and seek solutions rather than giving up in the face of difficulties.

Technology can also be a great ally in building an unstoppable sales team. Today, there are many digital tools that make salespeople's jobs easier, from customer relationship management (CRM) systems to sales tracking apps. These tools not only help organize information and save time, but they also provide valuable data that can be used to improve sales strategies. For example, by analyzing customer purchasing trends, the team can identify opportunities and adjust their approach to close more sales. Invest in technology that is easy to use and that really adds value to the sales process.

Finally, an unstoppable sales team needs a leader who inspires and guides them. A good leader is not just one who gives orders, but one who cares about the team's well-being, is involved in their training, and is willing to lead by example. Be a leader who is present, who knows his or her team, and who is willing to support them at all times. A leader who shows passion and commitment to the business inspires others to work with the same dedication. In addition, a leader must be able to adapt to changes and guide the team in new directions when necessary, always keeping a clear vision of the long-term objectives.

Building an unstoppable sales team is an ongoing process. It's not just about hiring people and expecting them to sell, but about creating an environment where each member feels motivated, valued, and equipped to do their best. It's a joint effort, involving investment in time, resources, and constant support. But in the end, a strong sales team is one of the best investments you can make to ensure your business not only survives, but thrives over the years. Because an unstoppable sales team doesn't just sell products; it builds relationships, represents the essence of the brand, and takes the business to new heights.

Adapting to Change in the Digital Age

Adapting to change is essential for any business that wants to last more than a hundred years, and in the digital age, this adaptation has become more important than ever. We live in times where technology advances by leaps and bounds and changes the way people buy, sell and communicate. What used to work to attract customers or sell products may be obsolete today. Therefore, one of the pillars of building a solid and lasting business is the ability to adapt to the technological and market changes that the digital age brings with it. It is not just about following trends, but being flexible and proactive enough to anticipate those changes and take advantage of them to benefit your business.

One of the most important aspects of adapting to change in the digital age is mindset. Companies that resist change tend to be left behind, while those that are open-minded and willing to try new ideas often thrive. The digital age has transformed the business world; from the way products are presented, to how customers are served. This can be intimidating, especially for more traditional businesses, but it is important to remember that technology is a tool that can make work easier, improve efficiency, and expand opportunities for growth. Adopting a mindset of constant learning and being willing to experiment with new tools and approaches is key to surviving and thriving in today's world.

Online presence is one of the most notable changes of the digital age. A few years ago, having a physical store was enough to reach customers, but today, if your business doesn't have an online presence, it's almost as if it doesn't exist. Today's consumers search for products and services online, research, compare prices, and read reviews before making a purchasing decision. That's why having a professional website and active social media profiles is no longer optional; it's necessary. A website allows people to learn about your business, your products, and your services from anywhere in the world and at any time of day. While social media is an excellent tool to interact with customers, resolve their doubts, and build a community around your brand.

Adapting to the digital age also means learning how to use the new tools that are available. Today, there are many technologies that can help improve a business's operations and increase sales. For example, customer relationship management (CRM) systems allow you to effectively organize and track customer interactions, helping to personalize service and build stronger relationships. E-commerce platforms make it possible to sell products online, reaching a much wider audience than you could reach with a brick-and-mortar store alone. Even messaging apps and chatbots make customer service easier, allowing you to answer questions and resolve issues quickly and efficiently. The challenge is being willing to invest time in learning how to use these tools and integrating them into your day-to-day business.

Data analysis is another key aspect of adapting in the digital age. Thanks to technology, it is now possible to collect and analyze a vast amount of information about customer behavior, market trends, and sales performance. Data is a goldmine for making more informed decisions and adjusting business strategies. For example, by analyzing social media metrics, you can find out what type of content generates the most interaction and what your followers' interests are. By reviewing sales statistics, you can identify which products are most popular and when they sell the most. By understanding customer patterns and preferences, you can create more effective marketing campaigns, improve products, and offer a more personalized service. The key is not to be afraid of data, but to see it as a powerful tool for improvement and growth.

But adapting to digital change isn't just about implementing technologies; it also involves understanding new consumer habits and expectations. Today's customers are more demanding, looking for fast, personalized, and convenient experiences. They want to be able to shop from their phones, receive notifications about deals, and ask questions via real-time chat. They also value companies that are transparent and authentic in their communication, that offer interesting and useful content, and that care about providing good service. That's why it's important for your business to stay alert to customer needs and preferences, and be willing to adjust its approach to meet them. Listening to what customers say on social media, reading their reviews, and asking for their feedback can offer valuable insights to improve the customer experience and adapt to what they're really looking for.

Another aspect of the digital age is the importance of innovation. Technology is constantly changing, and what is a novelty today may be a common tool tomorrow. To stay relevant in such a dynamic world, businesses must be willing to innovate, whether in the way they sell, the products they offer, or how they communicate with their customers. Innovating doesn't necessarily mean making big changes; sometimes small tweaks can make a big difference. For example, implementing a digital payment system in a physical store, offering free shipping on online purchases, or creating a mobile app to make the shopping experience easier. Continuous innovation shows that your business is up to date and cares about providing a modern and convenient service to its customers.

It's also important to recognize that adapting to digital change doesn't happen overnight. It's a gradual process that requires patience, learning, and sometimes making mistakes. The important thing is to start small, identifying the areas of your business that could benefit most from technology. Maybe the first thing is to create a website, then start selling online, or maybe improve customer service with a chatbot. The important thing is not to be paralyzed by the fear of change, but to take the first step and be willing to adjust course as needed.

Finally, adapting to change in the digital age means being proactive and always keeping an eye on new trends. Technology advances rapidly and the opportunities it offers are endless. Stay informed about market developments, new tools and best practices. Participate in courses, webinars and conferences, connect with other entrepreneurs and share experiences. Surrounding yourself with people and sources of information that are up to date with technology and the market will help you keep your business one step ahead. Remember that, in the digital age, the ability to learn and adapt is the best weapon to compete and continue growing.

Adapting to change in the digital age can be challenging, especially for more traditional businesses. But it is a necessary change to survive and thrive in a world where technology is present in every aspect of our lives. The good news is that by being willing to embrace new tools and approaches, you not only make your business more efficient, but you also open the door to new opportunities for growth. Technology is not the enemy; it is a powerful ally that, when used well, can help you build a stronger, more flexible business that is prepared for the challenges of the future.

Systems and Processes for Longevity

Systems and processes are the backbone of any business that seeks to last more than a hundred years. Having a great product or an unstoppable sales team is critical, but without solid systems to sustain day-to-day operations, the business runs the risk of becoming chaotic, inefficient, and eventually unsustainable. Systems and processes are like the cogs that keep everything running smoothly, efficiently, and consistently. They are what allow the business to function well, even when the founder is no longer in charge or when changes arise in the market. By designing effective systems, a business sets itself up for longevity, creating a solid foundation that can sustain it for generations.

When we talk about systems and processes, we are referring to the routines, steps, and rules that are followed to carry out daily operations. This can range from how a customer is served, how inventory is managed, how purchase orders are processed, to how staff is hired and trained. Having clear and well-documented processes not only makes tasks easier to perform, but it also ensures that things are done the same way every time, regardless of who is in charge. Consistency is key to maintaining the quality and reputation of the business over time.

One of the first steps to establishing effective systems and processes is to analyze how things are currently being done. Every business has a unique way of operating, but not all methods are the most efficient. Spend time observing and evaluating daily activities, from sales to customer service to inventory management. Ask yourself if there are unnecessary steps, if any tasks can be simplified, or if there are areas where mistakes are frequently being made. This initial analysis will give you a clear idea of where you can improve and what processes need to be adjusted or implemented.

Once you've identified the areas that need a system, the next step is to document how tasks should be performed. Documentation is critical to creating processes that are easy to follow and replicate. It's like an instruction manual that guides each team member through their work, ensuring everyone follows the same steps and maintains quality. When documenting processes, describe each step clearly and simply. For example, if you're creating a process for serving customers, detail everything from how to greet them, what questions to ask them, how to present products, to how to follow up after the purchase. The more specific you are, the easier it will be for others to follow the process correctly.

Technology can be a great ally when it comes to implementing systems and processes. Today, there are numerous digital tools that can help you automate and simplify many of your business operations. For example, an inventory management system can help you keep more precise control of your products, avoiding errors and losses. E-commerce platforms make it easier to take orders and track shipments, while a good customer relationship management system (CRM) allows you to effectively organize and track customer interactions. The key is to choose the tools that best fit the needs of your business and integrate them into your processes in a way that makes your job easier, rather than more complicated.

It's also important that your systems and processes are flexible and constantly under review. The market, trends and technology are constantly changing, so the processes that work today may not be the most effective tomorrow. Set aside time periodically to review how your systems are working and make adjustments where necessary. Talk to your team, listen to their feedback and see where the weak points or bottlenecks might be. For example, perhaps a customer service process that was once efficient is now slow due to increased inquiries. In this case, you could implement an online chat system or chatbot to streamline support and improve the customer experience.

Staff training is another crucial aspect when it comes to systems and processes. It's not enough to document and automate; your team needs to be trained and aware of the importance of following processes. Consistency is only achieved if everyone understands how and why things are done in a certain way. Provide ongoing training and make it clear that following processes is not just a rule, but a way to ensure quality and business efficiency. It's also important to create an environment where the team feels free to suggest improvements. Often, it's employees who notice small inefficiencies and can offer ideas for optimizing processes.

One system that can make a huge difference to the longevity of a business is the process of hiring and training staff. People are one of the most valuable assets of any company, and finding the right people is critical. Establishing a well-defined hiring process, including clear criteria for selecting candidates, specific tests and interviews, can help you build a stronger team. Additionally, a structured training process ensures that new employees understand the culture, values and expectations of the business from the start, allowing them to integrate more easily and perform their jobs effectively.

Standardizing processes also plays an important role in business expansion. A business that relies too much on one person to function becomes vulnerable. In contrast, when operations are based on clear processes, it is much easier to open new branches or delegate tasks to others. Imagine you want to expand your business to another city; if you have well-documented systems, you can train a new team in that city to follow the same procedures and maintain the same level of quality. This allows the business to grow without losing its essence or efficiency.

Another advantage of having clear systems and processes is that they make decision-making easier. When every aspect of your business is well organized and specific procedures are followed, you can have a clearer view of how things are working. Systems help you collect data and monitor performance, allowing you to identify patterns, problems, and opportunities. For example, if you have a well-structured process for tracking sales, you can spot if a product isn't selling as you expected and make informed decisions about whether to modify, remove, or promote it in a different way.

Systems and processes are not static; they must evolve along with the business. As the business grows, new needs and challenges are likely to arise. Maybe you need to add a new process to handle a larger volume of orders, or perhaps the marketing process needs to be adjusted to reach a new market segment. Flexibility is key to adapting systems to new circumstances, while maintaining efficiency and consistency at every stage of growth.

In short, systems and processes are essential to creating a strong business that can last for more than a hundred years. They are what allow operations to be carried out efficiently and the business to maintain its quality and reputation, no matter how many times team members or market conditions change. Although it may seem like tedious work at first, investing time in designing and implementing effective systems is one of the best decisions you can make to ensure the longevity of your business. Remember that a well-organized business is a business prepared to face the challenges of the future and to thrive throughout generations.

The Business Legacy

A business legacy is the set of values, principles, practices and contributions that a business leaves to the world and that defines it beyond its products and services. It is not just about the profits, the number of clients or the fame it has achieved. The true legacy of a company lies in the impact it has had on people's lives, on the community and on the sector in which it operates. A business that wants to last more than a hundred years must think about its legacy from the beginning, building something that goes beyond immediate results and inspires future generations. This legacy is what will allow the company to transcend time and remain relevant even when its founders are no longer there.

Building a business legacy means creating an identity and values that guide all of the business's decisions and actions. Values are the essence of the business, the way it behaves and relates to its customers, employees, partners, and community. They can include things like honesty, respect, innovation, quality, and social responsibility. When a business has clear values and consistently practices them, it earns people's trust and respect. That trust becomes a solid foundation on which to build a lasting legacy. Customers want to buy from companies that share their values and that act ethically and responsibly.

Legacy is also built through the mission and vision of the business. The mission is the purpose, the reason why the company exists. The vision, on the other hand, is the dream, the long-term goal of what the company wants to achieve and how it wants to be perceived in the future. Defining a clear mission and vision helps the company have a direction and motivation that goes beyond economic goals. For example, a company may have a mission to improve people's lives through innovative and sustainable products. With that mission in mind, all decisions will be made thinking about how they can contribute to that purpose. And by constantly working in that direction, the company begins to leave a mark, a legacy that reflects its commitment to its ideals.

The way a business treats its employees is also part of its legacy. A business that cares about the well-being of its team, provides them with opportunities for growth, and treats them with respect creates a positive environment that is reflected in the quality of work and customer service. Satisfied and motivated employees are more loyal and committed, and they are the ones who will help transmit the company's values and culture over time. In the end, a company is much more than a brand or a product; it is the people who make it up who truly bring it to life. When a company strives to be a good place to work, it is leaving a legacy of care, respect, and collaboration that inspires others and can be continued by the next generations.

Community engagement is another pillar of a business legacy. A business that engages and contributes to the well-being of the community creates bonds of support and trust that last. This can include activities such as participating in social development projects, supporting local organizations, implementing sustainable practices that care for the environment, or promoting education and economic development. By taking actions that benefit the community, the company demonstrates that it is not only interested in its own benefit, but seeks to make a positive difference in the world. Over time, these actions become a hallmark that distinguishes the company and that people remember and value.

A business legacy is also forged through innovation and the constant pursuit of excellence. A company that strives to improve, that dares to try new things and overcome challenges, inspires others to follow its example. It is not about innovating just to be fashionable, but about seeking solutions that really add value, that make people's lives easier or more pleasant. Innovation can be in products, services, processes or in the way of relating to customers. When a company becomes a pioneer in its sector and stands out for its creativity and quality, it is creating a legacy that influences the market and is recognized by others.

It is also important to think about business continuity as part of the legacy. A business cannot last a hundred years if it depends exclusively on one person or a small group. It must have a succession plan, a team that is prepared to take over when the founders are no longer there. Succession is not just a change of leadership, it is the transmission of the values, vision and culture of the company to the new generations. This process requires time and dedication; it involves training and coaching future leaders so that they understand and respect the essence of the company, but at the same time gives them the freedom to innovate and take the business towards new horizons. In this way, the company not only survives the change of people, but is strengthened and evolves with each new generation.

The products and services a company offers are also part of its legacy. When a company creates products that truly meet people's needs and desires, it leaves a mark on their lives. Think of those brands that have become part of people's history and memories, those that have products that are passed down from generation to generation. That emotional connection with products is a powerful part of a company's legacy. That's why it's important that products and services maintain a quality standard and reflect the company's values and identity. By doing so, the company earns a place in history and in the hearts of its customers.

Ultimately, a business legacy is the story that the business tells and leaves behind. It is the result of every decision, every action, and every word that has been said over time. It is what people will remember when they talk about the company in the future. That is why it is essential to act with integrity, think long-term, and not lose sight of the purpose and values that gave rise to the business. Building a legacy is not something that is achieved overnight; it is an ongoing process that is nurtured with every small action and that is forged over the years.

Leaving a legacy means creating something that has a lasting, positive impact on people, the community and the world. It's about giving more than you receive, inspiring and motivating others to keep going. A company with a strong legacy is one that has been adaptable, that has been true to its values and that has worked with passion and dedication to leave its mark. That legacy is what will make the business remembered and appreciated, and what will allow it to continue to grow and prosper for more than a hundred years. So, if you want to build a lasting business, don't just think about sales or profits. Think about the legacy you want to leave and work every day to build it.

www.ingramcontent.com/pod-product-compliance
Lightning Source LLC
Chambersburg PA
CBHW051227160726
47994CB00002B/775